CONFIRM YOUR FAITH

TO COMMEMORATE

....

of

....

in..

on...

by...

Confirm Your Faith

by

WILLIAM WESTON

Foreword by

THE RT REVD TIMOTHY BAVIN

The Canterbury Press
Norwich

Copyright © William Weston 1990

Published in this revised edition 1990
by The Canterbury Press Norwich
(a publishing imprint of Hymns Ancient & Modern Limited)
St Mary's Works, St Mary's Plain,
Norwich, Norfolk, NR3 3BH

*First published by the author in Australia
in 1974, reprinted (twice) 1975, 1977, 1978,
revised printing 1981 and reprinted 1984,
further revised printing 1989.*

British Library Cataloguing in Publication Data
Weston, William
Confirm your faith.
1. Church of England. Confirmation
I. Title
265.2
ISBN 1–85311–012–4

*Typeset by Eta Services, Suffolk
and printed in Great Britain by
St Edmundsbury Press, Suffolk*

Acknowledgement:

The Alternative Service Book 1980 *is copyright* © *The Central
Board of Finance of the Church of England. Extracts are
reproduced with permission.*

FOREWORD

IT IS OFTEN hard to find just the right book to put into the hand of those who have just been confirmed, but Bill Weston has written just such a book. With its concise treatment of a comprehensive range of subjects, it provides within a few pages (and at modest cost) the basic information which every Christian ought to know, but often does not.

To be able to provide a summary of Christian history in a dozen pages (including maps and illustrations) is no small feat and is the mark of an experienced teacher. He would be the first to admit, however, that his book provides but an outline of instruction in this, as in the other 16 chapters, and those who want to deepen their knowledge will need to read more widely. But many may well be moved to do so as a result of reading a book which is attractive to read and deceptive in its simplicity.

Nor should it be reserved for Confirmation candidates. It would make a splendid and inexpensive gift for people of all kinds and all ages, and our congregations would benefit enormously from having a grasp of the knowledge it contains.

So I hope that many will buy two copies of this book — one for themselves and one to give away. They will have cause to rise up and call its author blessed.

+ TIMOTHY PORTSMOUTH

This booklet is dedicated to the memory of
the Revd Canon Arthur Capell, D.Litt.
(28 March 1902–10 August 1986)

who spent much of his life establishing a means of communication with the newly discovered tribes of people in New Guinea where 750 different languages are spoken.

After gaining his Doctorate in Philosophy from the University of London in 1938, he became Reader in Oceanic Languages at the University of Sydney, where in 1981, on his 79th birthday, he was awarded its highest degree, *Doctor of Letters*, for his work in General Linguistics.

At the award ceremony he was described by the Vice Chancellor as 'a genius'. It was said that on one occasion Arthur went to a remote island in the Fiji group, and when he arrived in the morning he heard for the first time the completely different language which was spoken there. That evening he addressed a meeting of the people in their own language!

CONTENTS

The Bible

THE BIBLE IS a collection of many books written over a period of several hundred years.

Each book must be read in the light of the times when it was written. The writers were inspired by God, but they were limited by the environment of their times. They wrote about the progressive awareness in man of God's unchanging love, leading to the expectation of the revelation of God in his Messiah or Christ, the Hebrew and Greek titles for the one anointed for God's purpose.

The historical records are corroborated by those of surrounding nations, and archaeologists have verified many incidents described in the Bible.

The Old Testament

Genesis means beginning. The early chapters of Genesis contain the beautiful idea of creation for primitive people. They proclaim the eternal truth that all things came into being through the Word of God who made man in his own image, giving him freedom to choose right or wrong.

The rest of Genesis records the covenant made between God and Abraham and his descendants, concluding with the families of the sons of Abraham's grandson Israel, living in prosperity in Egypt.

God's Law

The Exodus story begins when the twelve families having grown into twelve tribes known as Israelites, have become slaves in Egypt. Exodus describes the call of Moses to lead the exodus of the Israelites from slavery; the origin of the Passover when they ratified their covenant with God by sacrificing a lamb to commemorate God's Angel passing over Egypt to set them free; their crossing of the Red Sea; their wandering in the wilderness and Moses receiving the Ten Commandments on Mount Sinai.

The Books of Leviticus, Numbers and Deuteronomy describe the development of the Law, the elaborate sacrificial system and the forty years journey to the border of the land promised by God to his people.

The Promised Land

The Books of Joshua and Judges record the settlement of the Promised Land, the strip of country at the eastern end of the Mediterranean Sea, from the Sea of Galilee in the north from which the River Jordan flows into the Dead Sea in the south.

The Book of Ruth is a beautiful story about the ancestors of David who became the greatest King in the Old Testament.

The books of Samuel, Kings and Chronicles give the historical account of the establishment of a monarchy, united under the kings Saul, David and Solomon who built the first Temple in Jerusalem. The land was divided into two separate Kingdoms in 936 B.C. with the Kingdom of Israel in the north, and the Kingdom of Judah in the south.

Prophets

In this period the prophets became prominent. They saw the hand of God in history. Apart from Obadiah denouncing the Edomites, the prophets were mainly concerned about the influence of the great powers of the day. The Northern Kingdom of Israel lay in the path of the expanding Assyrian empire. The prophets like Amos and Isaiah who revealed the justice and holiness of God, warned the people that they would lose their freedom because they had forsaken God's laws.

In 721 B.C. the doom foretold by the prophets came to pass when the Assyrians, whom the prophet Nahum denounced, annihilated the Northern Kingdom of Israel.

Jeremiah and Ezekiel, who emphasised each person's responsibility for his own sin, foretold the doom of the Kingdom of Judah as the power of Babylon replaced that of Assyria. In 586 B.C. the city of Jerusalem and the Temple were destroyed by the Babylonians and many of the people were carried off to Babylon. The Book of Lamentations is a dirge for the lost glory of Jerusalem.

The prophet Habakkuk who also bewailed the fall of Judah, expounded the doctrine to be developed later by St Paul, that the just shall live by faith.

The Exile

The Jews remained in exile in Babylon from 586 B.C. to 536 B.C. and developed into a worshipping community. During this period much of what we know as the Old Testament was collected and compiled.

King Cyrus of Persia conquered Babylon in 539

B.C. and allowed the Jews to return to their own land to rebuild Jerusalem and the Temple.

The Book of Daniel is a mystic book, describing the Exile and the fall of Babylon to the armies of Persia.

The books of Haggai, Zechariah, Ezra and Nehemiah have recorded the return from exile. The Old Testament reaches its peak in the book of Isaiah from the fortieth chapter onwards, which is full of the promises of the Messiah.

Esther is not a religious book. It describes the unity of the Jewish people during the Persian regime.

The other books include Psalms which are religious songs; Proverbs and Ecclesiastes which provide moral teaching; the Song of Songs, a wedding song which foreshadows the relationship between Christ and his bride the Church; Job, which deals with the problem of suffering; Hosea in which Israel is shown as the unfaithful wife of God who never ceases to love and forgive; Jonah in which the God of Israel is seen as the God of all people; Micah which reveals God's concern about social injustice; Zephaniah in which confidence in the guidance of God is emphasised. The Day of the Lord which Peter claimed was fulfilled when the Holy Spirit came to the Church is foretold in the Book of Joel. Malachi is the last book of the Old Testament which foretells the coming of the Sun of Righteousness preceded by his herald.

The Apocrypha

Between the Old Testament and the New Testament there is a group of books known as the Apocrypha, which means hidden or secret things.

These books give the history of the Jewish people when the Greeks under Alexander the Great, conquered the world, destroying the Persian Empire which had allowed the Jews religious freedom. Under the Greek regime the Jews were persecuted. The Apocrypha describes the courage of the Jews in their battles against their oppressors.

The New Testament

The New Testament contains the records of the fulfilment of the prophecies of the Old Testament in the coming of the Messiah or Christ who was named Jesus.

The four Gospel writers, Matthew, Mark, Luke and John have given their accounts of his teaching and his works through which the love of God was revealed in all its fullness, culminating in his death on the cross, his resurrection and ascension into Heaven.

The Acts of the Apostles is the sequel to St Luke's

The Gospel reading

(*Photo: Keith Ellis*)

13

Gospel, showing the amazing development of the Church as the body through which the work of Christ was continued through the lives of believers, after the coming of the Holy Spirit at Pentecost, fifty days after the resurrection.

This book reveals the expansion of the Church beyond the Jewish religion into the Gentile world, at first through the work of St Peter and then of St Paul who, before his conversion was Saul, the bitter enemy of the Church.

The Epistles are letters from certain leaders of the Church applying the teachings of Jesus to the various situations and problems in the life of the Church.

The last book, the Revelation of St John the Divine was written in symbolic terms to assure Christians who were facing bitter persecution at the hands of Nero the Roman Emperor, of the ultimate triumph of good over evil in the power of the risen and glorified Christ.

A Brief History of the Church

HISTORY CONFIRMS THE Bible's account in The Acts of the Apostles of the way the Church spread out from Jerusalem into all of the countries surrounding the Mediterranean Sea within a few years.

For nearly three hundred years the strongest force that the world had ever known tried to destroy Christianity. Thousands of Christians were killed by the Roman Government because they would not give up belief in Jesus Christ. The course of history changed in A.D. 321 when the faith Rome had tried to eliminate became the official religion of the Empire because the Emperor Constantine became a Christian.

Constantine encouraged Christianity and many people became Christians because it was fashionable.

Constantine moved the capital of the empire from Rome to the new city in the East, called after himself, Constantinople. It became one of five great centres of Christianity whose bishops assumed a status and prestige above all others. The others were the Bishops of Antioch, Jerusalem, Alexandria and Rome. These bishops were acknowledged as Patriarchs.

The Church Divided

Four of these cities were in the Eastern world, which was assailed and weakened by the Barbarians and later by the Moslems. Only Rome was in the West. Because of its political and commercial importance, those who successively held the office of Patriarch or Pope of Rome assumed more and more power.

In 1054 the Church on earth was divided into the Latin Catholic Church and the Eastern Orthodox Church because the Church in the east refused to recognise the claim of the Roman Patriarch to be the head of the whole Church on earth.

THE FIVE
PATRIARCHATES
IN 451

The Church of England

Christianity began in Britain soon after the death of Christ.

When Christianity became the religion of the Empire, local customs prevailed in the Church in Britain which was known as the Celtic Church. Easter was celebrated at a different time from the rest of the western world.

By A.D. 410 the Roman army of occupation had been withdrawn from Britain to protect Rome against the Barbarians. The undefended country was invaded by the fierce Angles, Saxons and Jutes who drove the British Christians to the west and north. The east of Britain was populated by the Anglo Saxons and the region became known as Angleland or England.

The old British Christians who, during this period produced many great saints, established a centre of missionary activity on the island of Iona off the west coast of Scotland. Under the leadership of St Columba missionaries were sent to convert the heathen English.

Columba died in A.D. 597 the year in which St Augustine arrived from Rome with a band of monks. They came to Kent and gained permission from the King of Kent to preach.

Augustine's mission spread from the east to the west, and Columba's from the north to the south and east. Gradually the two missions merged.

17

Because Augustine's mission had introduced the customs of the Church in Rome there was confusion. A meeting was held at Whitby in A.D. 664 at which it was decided to adopt the customs of the Western Church, such as the date of Easter, but the Church in England always maintained many of its own local traditions.

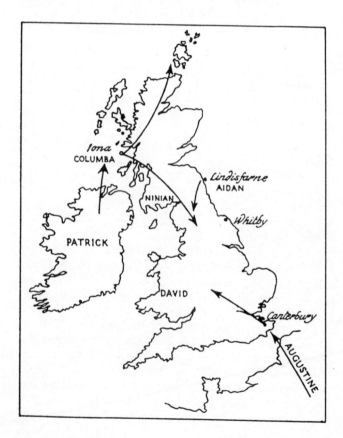

It may be said that at this time, what we now call the Church of England came into being from the union between the old Celtic Church and that introduced from Rome by St Augustine, who became the first Archbishop of Canterbury.

The Supremacy of The Pope

The Pope strengthened his authority over the rest of the Church in the western world, but the times were very insecure.

Hordes of fierce tribes of Barbarians, Huns and later the Moslems threatened the Roman Empire in which there were also internal disputes. For protection everyone gave allegiance to someone greater than himself in return for certain services. Those who were protected by a superior person became his vassals. The lord of the manor was the vassal of a higher noble who in turn, was the vassal of the King. Within the Empire were a number of Kingdoms whose rulers received their authority at the hands of the Emperor, who usually reigned in Italy.

In the reign of Pope Innocent III from 1198 to 1216 the power of the Pope was established over that of the Emperor and the Pope became the most powerful man in the world.

The Dark Ages

In the seventh century the teaching of the Prophet Mohammed spread very rapidly. The Mohammedans overran most of the eastern world and captured Jerusalem.

In the western world education was limited to very

few people. The monasteries were the only places where people could be taught.

When the Mohammedans threatened the sacred Christian shrines, a series of Crusades went from the west to protect them. The men returning from the Crusades brought back some of the lost culture from the east. About the same time the printing press was invented and more people learned to read. New ideas were circulated and the Renaissance, the rebirth of learning began.

The Reformation

In 1517, because Pope Leo X wanted money to complete St Peter's Cathedral in Rome, the sale of indulgences was inaugurated. By paying a fee for an indulgence, people were told that they could not only insure themselves against purgatory after death, but also free the souls of their dead relatives from the torments of purgatory.

A German monk named Martin Luther objected and rebelled against the Church. This was the beginning of the Reformation. Luther was followed by Zwingli and Calvin who were more extreme in their rigid interpretation of the Bible which people were learning to read.

A number of different churches were formed in Europe.

Some years before, in England a marriage had been arranged between Henry VIII and the Spanish princess Catherine of Aragon, the widow of Henry's older brother, by a Papal dispensation of Church law which forbade such a marriage.

Eighteen years later during which Henry VIII had denounced the European reformers, Henry realised that Catherine could never bear a male heir to the throne. He asked the Pope to annul his marriage because it had been a breach of Church law. At first the Pope agreed but pressure from Spain made him refuse.

Henry then had an Act of Parliament passed in 1534 repudiating any authority of the Pope in England. This did not create a new church. The marriage was annulled and Henry VIII married Anne Boleyn who became the mother of Elizabeth. Anne was later beheaded and Henry married Jane Seymour who died giving birth to a son who was to become Edward VI.

The First English Prayer Book

In Henry's reign the Latin services continued. The first Prayer Book in English was not produced until the second year of the reign of King Edward VI in 1549. This was a modified compilation of several Latin service books which had been in use.

Edward VI became king when he was only nine years old. He was advised by a Council of Regency with the notorious Somerset dominating the Council as Protector.

In Europe the Reformation brought into the open political feuds that had been brewing for many years. The Reformation not only split the Church, but divided Europe into two hostile camps, on one side were those who protested against the authority of the Pope and on the other, those who supported the Emperor and the Pope.

It seemed expedient to Somerset that England should support the powers behind the protestant reformers who were not satisfied with the first English Prayer Book. A second Prayer Book with strong protestant influence was produced in 1552 which advocated austere worship.

Somerset seized the opportunities provided by the 1552 Prayer Book to despoil the churches of many priceless treasures. These were days of anarchy in England and the boy King was a pawn in the hands of evil men.

The 1552 Prayer Book which had never received official sanction from the Church was not used widely, because Edward died in 1553. Mary, the daughter of Catherine of Aragon became Queen and restored the old Latin services. She decreed that the Pope was again to be recognised as the head of the Church of England.

Those who did not acknowledge the Pope were exiled, imprisoned or burned at the stake. One who was burned under Mary's orders was Archbishop Cramner of Canterbury who had produced the English Prayer Books. Mary died in 1557 after a reign of bitter religious turmoil and Elizabeth, the daughter of Anne Boleyn, became Queen.

The Elizabethan Age

Elizabeth regarded the Church of England as the same church which had always existed in England, but denied that the Pope had either lawful or scriptural authority.

In 1559 the third Prayer Book was produced modifying some of the changes made in the 1552 Prayer Book.

Those who still recognised the Pope's authority continued to attend the services in the Church of England until 1570 when the Pope withdrew them and sent Jesuit priests to establish the Roman Catholic Church in England.

The Puritans

The Puritans were people who were influenced by the teachings of John Calvin. Although they did produce some very devout people, their idea of religion was severe and rigid. Some remained within the Church of England, but others withdrew and almost succeeded in destroying it.

John Knox, who had been a chaplain to Edward VI was devoted to Calvin. On Edward's death Knox went to the Continent and returned to Scotland where he formed the Presbyterian Church as a church controlled by presbyters without bishops.

Throughout the reign of Elizabeth I the Church of England was assailed by both the Puritans and the Roman Catholics.

On the death of Elizabeth in 1603 the Kingdoms of Scotland and England were united when James VI of Scotland became James I of England.

In 1604 further additions were made to the Prayer Book to strengthen its teaching against Puritanism. The Authorised Version of the Bible, commonly known as King James Version, was produced in 1611.

Civil War

Church life was very vigorous during the next decades, but the Puritans eventually gained power in the Parliament.

James I was followed by Charles I whose reign was marked by a conflict with the Parliament which finally led to the Civil War in 1642.

The Puritan Parliament led by Oliver Cromwell, executed Archbishop Laud in 1645 in the attempt to destroy the Church of England. In 1649 Cromwell beheaded King Charles I, and for the next eleven years England was ruled by the Puritan Parliament.

Cromwell became the Protector of England. The Prayer Book was banned, bishops were exiled and clergy were deprived of their parishes.

In the years of Cromwell's rule more damage was done to church buildings by his men, than during the 1939–45 war.

The Restoration of the Monarchy

On Cromwell's death in 1658 he was succeeded by his son. Two years later England was glad to restore the monarchy with the return from exile of King Charles II. The bishops and clergy were reinstated and in 1662 the Prayer Book was revised bringing it closer to the Prayer Book of 1549.

Puritanism which had produced the Baptists, Congregationalists and the Quakers, suffered from the reaction which followed the Restoration and many went off to seek religious freedom in America.

The Church was attacked by worldliness. Bishops were appointed for political reasons, many clergy cared little for their people, and religion declined to an appalling state.

The Methodists

In 1729 an Anglican priest named John Wesley gathered a group of men at Oxford University. He challenged them to observe the rules of the Prayer Book. Because their lives became so methodically ordered, people called them 'Methodists'.

Wesley travelled the length and breadth of England, preaching in the open air about the redemption of man by Jesus Christ and thousands turned back to God.

After Wesley's death in 1791 his followers could not withstand the antagonism of the leaders of the Church of England. Contrary to his intentions, they withdrew and the Methodist Church was separated from the Church of England.

The Evangelical Revival

Wesley's preaching inspired men within the Church of England. His influence led to the Evangelical Revival which produced some great saints. Wilberforce

25

and the Earl of Shaftsbury abolished slavery and child labour and members of the Church became more aware of their responsibility to proclaim the Gospel in other lands.

The tide of Wesley's influence receded early in the nineteenth century into a further period of laxness. The clergy sadly neglected sacramental teaching. Many of them were badly trained. Some bishops said that the Church of England was folding her wings to die with what dignity she could. Nobody in authority seemed to care. Church buildings were left to rot and decay.

The Oxford Movement

In 1833 a group of men at Oxford University, John Keble, Henry Newman, Hurrell Froude and Edward Pusey began what is now called the Oxford Movement or the Catholic revival of the Church of England. These men saw that through the Apostolic ministry and sacraments, the Church of England was truly a part of the One Holy Catholic Church.

They faced bitter opposition, but inspired many young men and set England alight with the glorious commission of Christ to preach the Gospel in all the world. The great missionary societies flourished and some of the most brilliant and devout priests went to distant lands to proclaim the Gospel.

The party spirit which had divided the Church of England into what is commonly called High Church and Low Church since the influence of the Continental Protestants was intensified in the years that followed.

When some of the Revivalists attempted to restore the ornaments and the vestments as ordered by the Prayer Book, they were faced with extreme persecution. They were summoned before the civil courts and a number of clergy were even sent to prison for carrying out the teaching of the Prayer Book. In 1877, while his family starved, one of them was imprisoned for a year and seven months.

But crowds flocked into the churches of the clergy who were so bitterly persecuted by mobs, law courts and bishops. Gradually the cathedrals and most of the churches in England restored the vestments and their chancels to what they had been 'in times past', according to the order of the Prayer Book.

The Oxford Movement not only recalled Anglicans to an awareness of their Catholic heritage and sacramental life, but it also produced outstanding saints, men and women. Some of these joined the revived religious orders and took on tough pioneering jobs in the slums of the large cities, in the remote outposts of the old British Empire and in the new missionary areas which were growing rapidly.

The Anglican Communion

Within the Anglican Communion there are now about five hundred dioceses in over twenty self governing churches which originated from the Church of England. New dioceses are being formed especially in the younger churches. There is a continuous increase in the number of Christians in the developing nations in Africa.

All of these churches acknowledge the primacy of the Archbishop of Canterbury, who presides when their bishops gather in England for the Lambeth Conference every ten years.

Most of the churches within the Anglican Communion developed from the 16th century Elizabethan age when exploration began from England, but two centuries were to pass before a bishop was consecrated for work beyond Britain.

Therefore from the 16th century to the 18th century clergy had to be imported to minister to those who had settled in the new colonies, and only colonists who could return to England were able to be confirmed.

The latter part of this period was a bad era for the Church of England. When James II was deposed in 1689 by Parliament, the Archbishop of Canterbury with eight other bishops and 400 priests withdrew because they could not swear allegiance to William and Mary while James was still living. They were called Nonjurors and began a division in the Church which lasted until 1805.

During this period attempts were made to send a bishop to America, but the legislature in England presented problems for the consecration of a bishop for a region beyond England. There was also opposition from those who had sought religious freedom in the New World who associated bishops with the ruling classes who had persecuted them.

For these reasons, the first bishop to be consecrated for overseas Anglicanism was consecrated in 1784 for North America by the bishops of the Episcopal Church of Scotland.

The English legislation was overcome and the first bishop to be consecrated in England for overseas work was consecrated for Canada in 1787.

During the next fifty years, bishoprics were created for Quebec in 1798, Calcutta, a diocese which included Australia, in 1813, Jamaica and Barbados in 1824, Madras in 1835, Australia in 1836 and Bombay in 1837.

Progress was quicker in the next few years as new dioceses were established in Canada, America, on the continent of Africa, Australia, New Zealand, West Indies and South East Asia including China, Korea and Japan.

In the middle of the 19th century, missionary work flourished through the influence of the growing missionary societies like the Society for Promoting Christian Knowledge (S.P.C.K.) which had been founded in 1698, the Church Missionary Society (C.M.S.) founded 1799, The Society for the Propagation of the Gospel (S.P.G.) founded 1701 and the University Mission to Central Africa (U.M.C.A.) founded 1857. The last two were amalgamated recently to become the United Society for the Propagation of the Gospel (U.S.P.G.).

Due to the work of these organisations and many others, by the beginning of the twentieth century the Anglican family of churches had become one of the greatest missionary forces in the world.

The great tragedy of Christianity is still its divisions, which must grieve Our Lord who founded the Church to be the body through which he would continue his work.

During the past few years there has been a greater awareness of the need for Christian unity, and churches of all denominations are working together and praying together as never before in human history.

The Ministry

THE WORD *minister* comes from a Latin word meaning *one who serves*. All Christians are called to be ministers, but some are called to serve as ordained ministers. At first Jesus called men and women to be disciples and from these he chose twelve men and ordained them to be apostles. The word *disciple* means a learner or pupil. The word *apostle* comes from a Greek word meaning *one sent with a mission*. On the first Easter evening Jesus ordained the Apostles with the same authority the Father had given him. 'As my Father has sent me, so I send you.'

Acting on this authority, the Apostles set apart seven men by the laying on of their hands to assist in serving the needy.

The word *deacon* comes from a Greek word which also means *servant*. Ordained servants are called deacons.

When the Church began to grow, senior men or eldermen were set apart by the laying on of the Apostles' hands to have charge of local churches. They were called *presbyters* from the Greek word for elder. The word *presbyter* became *priest*. So in the New Testament Church, the ordained ministry consisted of the Apostles, the Elders (priests) and the Deacons.

Another word also appeared. This was *bishop* from a Greek word *episcopos* meaning an *overseer*. Certain priest-elders like Titus and Timothy were given oversight of certain areas with authority to ordain (Titus 1.5).

They became the prototype of bishops as we know them today. Only bishops can administer confirmation and ordination. When the Apostles died, the Bishops succeeded them and the ordained ministry of Bishops, Priests and Deacons was left.

Those who enter the ordained ministry are first made deacons through the laying on of hands by a bishop. The deacon's work is limited. Deacons may assist the priests in the administration of Holy Communion, but they do not have authority to bless the bread and wine to be the body and blood of Christ. Deacons may read the Scriptures, teach young people, baptise when a priest is unavailable and preach if the Bishop gives permission. Deacons are also required to seek out the sick and needy in their parishes and inform the priest. Deacons appointed to progress to the Order of Priesthood have usually served as deacons for about a year then, through the laying on of the Bishop's hands, they are ordained priests. In this service other priests join in the laying on of hands with the Bishop who repeats the words of Jesus on the first Easter evening after he had given the Apostles the same authority the Father had given to him — in the words of *The Alternative Service Book 1980* Ordination service, 'Send down the Holy Spirit upon your servant for the office and work of a priest in your Church.' Then the bishop says:

> 'Almighty Father, give to these your servants grace and power to fulfil their ministry among those committed to their charge; to watch over them and care for them; to absolve and bless them in your name, and to proclaim the gospel of your salvation. Set them among your people to offer with them spiritual sacrifices acceptable in your sight and to minister the sacraments of the new covenant. As you have called them to your service, make them worthy of their calling. Give them wisdom and discipline to work faithfully with all their fellow-servants in Christ, that the world may come to know your glory and your love.'

How this authority is used is explained in the chapter on Forgiveness. Only those who have received the Order of Priesthood may conduct the service of Holy Communion.

A parish is an area in which people live, around a church. A priest appointed to have the cure or care of the souls of the people in a parish is called the rector or vicar.

The word *rector* comes from a Latin word for ruler. A rector is the spiritual ruler of the parish. The word *vicar* comes from a Latin word *vicarius* meaning deputy. The vicar originally was the deputy of a person like the lord of the manor or an establishment like a monastery or university having the right to appoint a priest to a parish. Today rectors and vicars usually have the same authority. They may be assisted by priests and deacons as assistant curates.

Groups of parishes in the same area form a diocese over which a bishop has oversight. Several dioceses in the same country or state make up a province.

The Bishop of the senior diocese in a province is called an archbishop. The presiding Bishop or Archbishop of an independent church in the Anglican Communion is called a primate or primus.

In England the Prime Minister nominates priests to the Sovereign to become bishops, but in most other parts of the Anglican Communion, priests are elected by synods or special committees to be consecrated as bishops.

When a priest has been appointed to be a bishop, at least three bishops join in the act of consecration through the laying on of their hands.

The Archbishop or senior consecrating Bishop says, 'Send down the Holy Spirit upon your servant – for the office and work of a bishop in your Church.'

The main church in a diocese is called a cathedral, because it contains the cathedra or chair of the Bishop.

The priest in charge of a cathedral is called the Dean.

Priests who have seats on the governing body of a Cathedral, which is the Chapter, are called canons. A canon may be the rector or vicar of a parish, but he uses his title, Canon. In the early church the administrative work was done by deacons and the chief deacon administrator was called an archdeacon. Today archdeacons are priests who assist the Bishop in the administration of the Diocese.

Those ordained to the ministry act within the authority of the whole church but all Christians should regard what they do every day as service to God.

Forgiveness

BY SIN THE relationship between God and man is broken. Forgiveness is the restoration of the relationship.

The death of Jesus Christ shows how far God has gone to restore the relationship. On the first Easter night, when Jesus said to his Apostles, 'Whose sins you forgive they are forgiven, whose sins you retain they are retained,' he showed that the ministry of forgiveness was to be a major part of the work of his Church on earth.

To be forgiven, we must accept what Christ has done for us and confess our sins.

If we need guidance or reassurance about forgiveness, we should confess our sins in the presence of a priest and receive from him counsel and absolution.

'Let him come to me, or to some other discreet and learned Minister of God's Word, and open his grief . . .' (Book of Common Prayer)

Some find it a helpful discipline to do this regularly.

The Prayer Book, in the service for the Visitation of the Sick, provides for confession of sin in the presence of a priest, who will, with Christ's authority, give absolution. No priest under any circumstances can reveal anything that is heard in a confession.

Often the need of this ministry is realised as the result of a deep spiritual experience, or a crisis, despair, remorse or guilt.

All of the regular services provide for a general confession with absolution, which can only be pronounced by a priest.

Forgiveness is freely offered. Our part is to know that we have been forgiven.

Christian Belief

THERE ARE THREE Creeds: The Apostles' Creed which is a bold statement of belief; the Nicene Creed which originated at Nicea in A.D. 325 to safeguard the Church against wrong teaching about the divinity of Christ; and the Creed of St Athanasius who led the Council of Nicea to the right decision. His Creed is really a song of triumph springing from belief in the revelation of God as the three persons of the Holy Trinity—Father, Son and Holy Spirit.

The Creeds express the way God has revealed himself to mankind.

God is the creator whom man learned to know as the Father, because he brought man into being and sustained his life.

The agent of the Creator, described as the Word of God or the Son of God, took humanity in a period of time to reveal God's love to man. He who had always existed did not need an earthly father. He was born of the Virgin Mary according to the will of God, not of man. The love and power of God coming from the Father and the Son is described as the Holy Spirit.

In the Creeds the Church professes belief in the great acts of God, which reveal the Trinity in unity. These are the Creation; the Incarnation which is God becoming man; the Crucifixion; the Resurrection; the Ascension and the Coming of the Holy Spirit to give life to the Church.

The Church consists of a body of people who, by the power of the Holy Spirit, are living in unity with Christ. The Church is described as One because unity is essential to the nature of Christ; it is holy because it is set apart for God's purpose; it is catholic because it is universal, for all people everywhere; and it is apostolic

35

because it was founded upon the Apostles who were sent into all the world.

The Holy Spirit guides the Church and, through the Communion of Saints, links together in it God's people on earth with those who have passed from this life. The Holy Spirit is the agent of Christ in the forgiveness of sins and the life-giving power who will raise us at the resurrection of the dead, in the life of the world to come.

The profession of faith reaches its conclusion as we say Amen, so be it. So we affirm our acceptance of what we have professed.

As we reach this climax, Jesus Christ, our Lord, stands before us; crucified, glorified, reaching out his arms to draw us to himself, the way, the truth, the life, the beginning, the end, the same yesterday, today and forever.

And as we say the great Amen, we know that the prayer of the divine Son of God who took our humanity will be answered in us, that we may be united with him in the glory of the Father, through the power of the Holy Spirit.

Baptism

THE GIFT OF eternal life, bought for us by Our Lord's death on the cross, is given to us as individuals through the sacrament of Baptism.

Jesus commanded his Apostles to make disciples of all nations, baptising in the Name of the Father, and of the Son, and of the Holy Ghost all who would repent and accept His sacrifice for their sins.

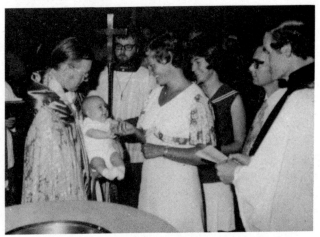

'We Welcome You'

At first those baptised were adults, but there is no record in the New Testament of the refusal of the Church to baptise children. There is evidence of whole families, which could have included children, being baptised, and in time it became the general practice to baptise the infants of Christian parents.

The order of service in the Church of England's *The Alternative Service Book 1980* is as follows:

> The duties of parents and godparents are stated; parents and godparents signify their willingness to help and encourage by their prayers, example and teaching those about to be baptized; the teaching of Jesus and the Apostles about baptism is then stated; the parents and godparents are required on behalf of the child, to declare that they 'turn to Christ', repent of their

sins, and renounce evil; the water in the font is then set apart with a prayer . . . 'that your *servants* who *are* washed in it may be made one with Christ in his death and delivered from all sin . . . bring *them* to new birth in the family of your Church, and raise *them* with Christ to full and eternal life'; parents and godparents are required to declare their belief and trust in God the Father, in his Son Jesus Christ, and in his Holy Spirit; naming the child, the priest pours water over the child's head, and says 'I baptize you in the name of the Father, and of the Son, and of the Holy Spirit'; a cross is signed on the forehead of the child who is then received into the Church, all present saying 'We welcome you into the Lord's family . . .'; finally prayers are offered that those who have been baptized 'may grow in the faith', that their parents be given 'the spirit of wisdom and love; and 'that their *homes* may reflect the joy of your eternal kingdom'.

Adults who are baptised should understand the Christian Faith. Before their baptism they should confess their sins. They should be confirmed as soon as possible, after being baptised.

Baptism represents the death, burial and resurrection of Our Lord. It also represents the death of the sinful nature which we inherit from all mankind, the burial of that nature as we were covered by the water, and the resurrection to new life as members of Christ's Church as children of God and inheritors of the Kingdom of Heaven.

Confirmation

THE PURPOSE OF Confirmation is to strengthen, by the power of the Holy Spirit, the new life which was given in Baptism.

In the first part of the service those who are to receive the laying on of the Bishop's hands, confirm the vows made by their parents and godparents, to renounce evil, and to believe the teachings of the Church.

The Bishop prays that those upon whom he will lay his hands will receive the outpouring of the Holy Spirit, so that they will have Wisdom to love God, Understanding of the presence of God in their lives, Knowledge of the true faith, Counsel to know God's will, Inner Strength to do it, Godliness that they may grow Godlike in character, and Holy Fear which is wonder and awe in God's presence, that they will love him so much that they will fear to grieve him by what they may do or fail to do.

As a successor of the Apostles, who sent Peter and John to lay their hands on those whom Philip the deacon had baptised in Samaria (Acts 8.14–17), it is the Bishop's function to administer confirmation. Those who are to be confirmed come forward and the Bishop lays his hands on their heads, following the example of the Apostles. Then he prays that they will be defended with the Grace of God and daily increase in his Holy Spirit.

When the Apostles received the Holy Spirit ten days after Jesus had ascended into Heaven, they felt the exhilaration of being filled with the same power which had been in Jesus, and which could never be separated from Jesus.

This is the power which is given in Confirmation.

In the service of Holy Communion, the great affirmation is made, 'We are the Body of Christ'. We justify this affirmation when we say, 'His Spirit is with us'.

The Bishop prays that those whom he confirms will daily increase in the Holy Spirit. In the Holy Communion service we pray to be renewed.

The Holy Spirit is the guiding hand of God.

Our Lord has given us the promise that when we are confronted with a difficult situation without any time for premeditation, the Holy Spirit will guide us. 'But whatsoever shall be given you in that hour, that you will speak, for it is not you who speak, but the Holy Spirit (Mark 13.11).

At such times we should simply say, 'Holy Spirit guide me'. The guidance will always be given.

The New Testament emphasises that the greatest evidence of the reception of the Holy Spirit is the service rendered to others through the transformed life of the receiver.

Holy Communion

The New Covenant

THE NEW COVENANT between God and man which was ratified by the obedient life, the death, resurrection and ascension of Our Lord, is perpetuated for us in the service of Holy Communion.

When Our Lord instituted the service at the Last Supper he anticipated the sacrifice he would offer next day for the sins of all mankind. What he anticipated, we commemorate until his coming again, as he has commanded us. In this way we accept what he has done for us, and receive the benefits of his sacrifice.

These benefits are communion or unity with Christ as he is now, triumphant over death and glorified by his resurrection and ascension; the realisation of his presence with us as he dwells in us and we dwell in him; unity with those who are united with him, and the hope of what shall be, according to his promise that those who eat his flesh and drink his blood possess eternal life and will be raised up at the last day (John 6.54).

The Offertory

In the service of Holy Communion we make a gift of money which represents the offering of our life and work to God. The money is offered with the bread and wine, symbols of life and joy, which have been processed from the fruits of the earth by our work.

Nothing that we can offer is worthy of God, but our gifts are offered in our commemoration of the most perfect offering ever made, the complete, perfect sacrifice of Christ himself on the Cross. We offer our sacrifice of praise and thanksgiving. The service is often

The priest consecrating the bread and wine at the Eucharist.
(Photo: Paul Skirrow)

called the Eucharist, from the Greek word for thanks-giving.

Participation

Only a priest has the authority of the Church to bless the bread and wine to be set apart as the body and blood of Christ, and to give absolution from sin, but in these days there is a greater emphasis on the participation of the laity as servers, readers, and in the administration of the Sacrament to the people.

Holy Communion is the Sacrament of unity. The spirit of our worship should be revealed in the way we express our unity with God and man in the daily life of the world.

Christian Stewardship

CHRISTIANS SHOULD SHOW their love of God both in acts of worship and in loving service to all in need.

The minimum observance of worship should be attendance at Church every Sunday, preferably at the service of Holy Communion, with daily prayer and Bible reading. Some are able to attend week day services, especially on Holy Days and during Lent.

We should also be aware of our duty to God and to our neighbours in all that we do every day.

It is our duty to give a portion of our time, ability and money in gratitude for what God has given to us. People are often surprised when they discover just how often Jesus referred to money and other possessions in His parables. He always tried to raise the level of human thought so that people would consider their possessions as being entrusted to them by God.

We should support the Church financially as we are able. The most efficient way is through a weekly envelope. Our offering should represent a sacrificial portion of our income, however the percentage of money we give to God is not as important as how we use what is left. God is not concerned so much about the proportion of spare time we give to the Church, but how we spend all of our time. The purpose of our stewardship is to develop a worshipping community in which we offer our time, ability and money to enrich the world with the life of Christ.

We must be concerned about the rights of others, especially in opposing racism and social injustice.

Christian service will involve us in every aspect of life, in the support of missionary work, of under-privileged children, of the sick, the bereaved, and lonely old people. Many opportunities of service will present themselves in the normal routine of daily life.

All of us who are sincerely involved in Christian service should ask whether God may be calling us to give the whole of our life in his service at home or in the mission field.

We should ask again and again—'What does God want me to do with what people call mine—my time—my money—my life?'.

James, John and Louise, Leaders of a Durham Cathedral Camp, make plans for the week's voluntary work.

(Photo: courtesy of 'The Journal', Newcastle)

Marriage

The Alternative Service Book 1980 service reminds us that marriage is 'a gift of God in creation and a means of his grace, a holy mystery in which man and woman become one flesh. It is God's purpose that, as husband and wife give themselves to each other in love throughout their lives, they shall be united in that love as Christ is united with his Church.'

The service recalls that Christ beautified marriage by performing his first miracle at the wedding in Cana, when he turned the water into wine.

The bride and bridegroom are solemnly warned that they must not enter into the state of matrimony merely for their own selfish reasons, but to consider very carefully the reasons why God himself ordained this holy estate.

A wedding is a welding together of two people into a family unit through which children can be brought into the world and nurtured in the Christian Faith.

Marriage enables the natural physical or sexual instincts to be directed in the right way. The Church teaches that sex directed in the right way is a holy gift of God, through which the full beauty of the love between a husband and a wife can be expressed.

Another reason for marriage is for the mutual society, help and comfort that the husband and wife should have for each other in prosperity and adversity. This means that marriage is a sharing of common interests in life.

The bride and bridegroom make very solemn vows to each other, to have and to hold each other under all conditions until they are parted by death.

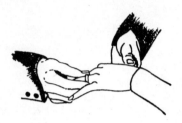

The vows are sealed by giving and receiving a ring as the outward visible sign of the holy love of God which has united them, and they receive the blessing of God as the priest pronounces them man and wife.

The second part of the service begins as the bride and bridegroom kneel for the prayers for their life together.

The people present, who have been witnesses in the first part of the service, now join with the bride and bridegroom in prayers for them.

The Prayer Book recommends that the service of Holy Communion should follow. It is most fitting that, as the couple have been joined to each other, they should be united with Our Lord through the Sacrament of his body and blood.

Married life certainly has its problems. It is easier to fall in love than to remain in love, but those who sincerely want to make their marriage all they hope it will be as they leave the church on their wedding day, should continually keep in touch with the God who is love and who gave them their love.

Private Prayer

OUR CONCEPT OF prayer is very limited if we only use it as a last resort in times of distress. Times of happiness and joy should also lead us to prayer, with thanksgiving.

Jesus prayed regularly to his Father. If prayer was necessary for him, it is essential for us.

Prayer is really being aware of God's presence. When we realise this we can pray anywhere, but it is best to set aside a certain time each day for prayer.

Set prayers are helpful because they can direct our thoughts. If our minds wander, we should pray about the things to which they wander.

Systematically we should pray for others; our loved ones; those in trouble, sickness or need. We should pray for ourselves; for our needs; for forgiveness as we confess our sins, praying for those we have wronged. If we have pressing desires, good or bad, certainly we should pray about them.

Prayer should include Bible reading and meditation. It is good to use a guide, such as the notes supplied by the Bible Reading Fellowship which help us to read the Bible intelligently and to meditate on what we have read.

Prayer life is incomplete without regular worship in God's house with the company of other members of God's family.

The Bible teaches us to pray to the Father, through Jesus Christ Our Lord in the power of the Holy Spirit.

An essential ingredient of prayer is faith. Sometimes our faith seems weak. We pray through Jesus Christ whose faith never waivered and he taught us that God's will is supremely good. Therefore, because we pray through Jesus Christ, we can lean on his strong faith.

Common Prayer

THE PRAYER BOOK is called the 'Book of Common Prayer' because the services it contains are common, for everyone. Some of these are regular services, others are occasional services.

Also, *The Alternative Service Book 1980* is authorised for use in the Church of England. The regular services are Morning and Evening Prayer and Holy Communion (also called The Eucharist and The Lord's Supper).

The occasional services which are used for special occasions include Baptism, Confirmation, Marriage, the Visitation of the Sick, the Burial of the Dead and the services for the Making, Ordaining, and Consecrat-

Prayers of Intercession at the Eucharist, St Faith's, Great Crosby, Merseyside.

(Photo: Paul Skirrow)

ing of Bishops, Priests and Deacons. All of these services have their authority from the Bible.

From the Prayer Book we can discover four features of our corporate worship.

The first is that we have set forms of prayer because prayers cannot be 'common' unless everyone joins in the same prayers.

The second feature is the historical background of our services. Although the first Prayer Book was produced in English in 1549, it was a compilation of a number of ancient service books. The services of Morning and Evening Prayer are like the services Our Lord attended in the Synagogue. The Service of Holy Communion is the service he gave us himself.

Thirdly, our worship is congregational because everyone can take part in it.

Fourthly, our worship is biblical. Almost every phrase in the services comes from the Bible, and the regular services of Morning and Evening Prayer and Holy Communion contain systematic Bible readings.

The Ministry to the Sick

THREE FACTS STAND out from the accounts of the Healing Miracles of Our Lord. The first is that he had compassion on all sufferers. The second is that Jesus frequently attributed healing to the faith of the sufferers themselves, or to the faith of others who were concerned about them. The third is that what Jesus did could be done in His name by those who had faith in him, only if they were in unity with each other.

Healing miracles declined when bitterness divided the Church.

In recent years there has been a revival of the Ministry of Healing which significantly coincides with the growth of Christian Unity.

Jesus said that the works he did would be done by believers, and that the works would be greater because of his return to the Father. His purpose was that the Church should continue his works, making them greater because of their availability wherever there were believers throughout all ages.

Our Lord told his disciples to anoint the sick with oil. St James in his epistle says that the anointing should be administered by the clergy with the prayer of faith and confession of sin.

The chapter on Forgiveness has shown that the service for the Visitation of the Sick provides for confession of sin to a priest.

Many people sick in body or soul have experienced great help by receiving absolution after confession and physical illness has often been healed.

The ministry to the sick should be a normal part of parish life. Concerned people should always tell their clergy of cases of illness.

In many churches special services are held in which the sick are prayed for, and in which the laying on of hands is administered to the sick or to those who in this way make an act of faith on behalf of the sick for whom they pray. An abundance of wonderful blessings has been the consequence.

All healing comes from God. The Ministry of the Church should support the work of the medical profession to effect the purpose of God for the wholeness of men, women and children.

The Christian Year

THE CHRISTIAN YEAR is divided into two parts. The great acts of God for man are commemorated in the first half, and in the latter we are taught how we should respond to what God has done for us.

By this means every aspect of the Christian Faith receives its due emphasis and the whole of the Faith is presented every year.

The Calendar also provides variety and continuity.

Every Sunday has special readings from the Bible with a Collect which collects the theme of the readings into a prayer.

As we join in the same celebrations year by year we are linked with the life of the Church stretching back to those events which are celebrated.

Advent

The first great act of God which is celebrated is the Incarnation. Incarnation means 'in the flesh'. In the Messiah or Christ whom the prophets of the Old Testament foretold, God became incarnate, taking human flesh and human nature. The Christian year begins four Sundays before Christmas with the Advent Season when we prepare to celebrate the first Advent of Christ. We also contemplate his second Advent when he shall come in glory to judge the world.

Advent is a penitential season because the sin of mankind made the first Advent of Christ necessary.

Christmas

On Christmas Day the Church celebrates the humble birth of Christ in Bethlehem, born of the Virgin Mary. If we believe that he whose birth we celebrate was God, it is impossible not to believe in the virgin birth. He who had always existed needed no earthly father because his birth did not depend upon the will of man, but of God. However, he did need an earthly mother to take our humanity.

The Epiphany

The Christmas season lasts for twelve days until the Feast of the Epiphany which falls on 6 January.

Epiphany means to manifest. On the Feast of the

Epiphany the manifestation of Christ to the Wise Men who followed the star is commemorated.

The number of Sundays after Epiphany is determined by the date of Easter. On each one an example of the manifestation of the glory of God in Jesus is given in the Bible readings. These Sundays and those which follow Trinity Sunday are now called ordinary Sundays.

Lent

The Lenten Season was the old English expression for Spring, when the days lengthen.

The first day of Lent is called Ash Wednesday because of the custom of the imposition of ashes on the heads of worshippers as a symbol of fasting.

Lent begins with the Commemoration of Our Lord's fast in the wilderness for forty days, but concludes with the commemoration of His passion and death. Notable days in Lent are Mothering Sunday on the fourth Sunday, Passion Sunday when the emphasis is focused on the sufferings of Christ, Palm Sunday, the first day of Holy Week when Jesus' triumphant entry into Jerusalem is commemorated, Maundy Thursday when the sacrament of Holy Communion was given. Maundy refers to the new commandment to love one another. The climax of Holy Week is Good Friday, the day of the Crucifixion.

Jesus' descent into hell is remembered on Easter Eve. While his dead body lay in the tomb Jesus in the Spirit went to the place of the dead (which in the words of the Book of Common Prayer version of the Creed is called hell, not meaning the place of ultimate separation from God as we understand Hell today).

Easter

The greatest event in the history of the world is the Resurrection of Jesus Christ. Easter is the most important festival of the Church when every confirmed person is obliged to receive Holy Communion. Because Jesus showed himself alive after his death for forty days, the season lasts for forty days.

The Ascension

On the fortieth day after the Resurrection, Jesus, in his recognisable human body, ascended into Heaven, having sent his Apostles into the world promising to send them the Holy Spirit to enable them to continue his work of salvation.

Pentecost (Whitsuntide)

Ascensiontide lasts for ten days because after our Lord's ascension the Apostles waited for ten days for the fulfilment of his promise to send the Holy Spirit.

On the Feast of Pentecost when the Jews gave thanks for the fruit of the earth, fifty days after the Passover, the Holy Spirit came to the Apostles appearing like fire on their heads, enabling them to proclaim the mighty works of God in different languages. Three thousand people were baptised and it became the custom to baptise new converts at this time each year. Because so many wore white robes, the Feast of Pentecost was also called White Sunday or Whitsunday.

Trinity

The Feast of the Trinity, one week after Whitsunday, does not commemorate an event like the festivals in the first half of the year, but a teaching of the Church about the nature of God who has revealed himself as the Trinity.

The best word which man could use to describe the separate identities of the One God is person. Each person of the Godhead—Father, Son and Holy Ghost, is distinct, yet united in nature, will and action.

The number of Sundays after Trinity in the Prayer Book (or after Pentecost in the ASB) varies with the date of Easter, but on each of them the Church teaches how we should apply the Christian Gospel to daily life.

Holy Days

Certain days are set apart to commemorate the lives of men and women who have enriched the world with the life of Christ.

Colours are used in church adornments to designate the season and festivals.

White or gold is used for Great Festivals and joyful times; Red for the fire of the Holy Spirit at Pentecost or for the blood of a saint who suffered martyrdom; Violet (or known as purple) for the penitential seasons of Advent and Lent, and Green, the colour of nature, for the Sundays after Epiphany and Pentecost which are the ordinary seasons.

Fifteenth century Russian icon of Christ Pantocrator—enthroned as the all-ruling Lord of the universe.

(Photograph Courtesy of Temple Gallery, London)

Beyond Earthly Life

THE BIBLE TEACHES that death is an event in life as the soul goes on to its eternal destiny.

The texts from the Bible accompanying the following statements should be read with the statement and carefully considered.

It is God's will that all mankind should be saved (1 Timothy 2.4).

Heaven is the house of God in which there are many rooms (John 14.2 and Psalm 23.6).

Jesus has ascended to prepare a place for all who accept his life (John 14.2a, 3).

Heaven is beyond our human understanding (1 Cor. 2.9).

We must all be judged (Rom. 14.10), but those who have followed Christ will not be condemned (John 3.16), and will have everlasting life (John 5.24 and 6.51).

Those who die in ignorance, unable to help themselves will be in peace (Luke 16.19–22).

There is a place for those who have unknowingly served Christ through their service to others (Matthew 25.40).

Immediately after his death Our Lord went to the place of departed spirits (1 Peter 3.19). Jesus called it Paradise (Luke 23.43).

Paradise is not Heaven because Jesus did not go to Heaven until the fortieth day after he rose from the dead (Acts 1.2–3).

In the place of departed spirits, the dead can remember this life and recognise those with whom they shared it (Luke 16.25).

This memory may cause spiritual pain because the

dead see themselves as this life made them (Luke 16.25). This revelation can lead to spiritual progress through a growing concern for others (Luke 16.28).

Before Christ's death the spirits of those who had disobeyed the law of love were imprisoned by an uncrossable gulf (Luke 16.26). After his death Jesus preached to the imprisoned dead (1 Peter 3.19 & 4.6) having bridged the gulf by his cross.

The faithful departed cannot attain perfection without us (Heb. 11.40).

The spirits of those willing to be justified by Christ make spiritual progress to perfection (Hebrews 12.23). They are led to the state of complete fulfilment (Rev. 7.17).

Those who enter Heaven will receive a body suitable for the Heavenly environment (1 Cor. 15.49).

Those who freely reject God will be in Hell, simply because they will not be with God (John 3.19).

We are united in the Communion of Saints with the faithful departed who are witnesses to us of salvation (Heb. 12.1).

Conclusion

As we desire what is good for those whom we love in this life, it is right and natural that we should express in prayer our great hope for their eternal good on the other side of death.

In the Burial service we express this hope and pray that we, with our departed loved ones, may attain perfect fulfilment and joy.

Worship and Service

JESUS TAUGHT THAT the worship of God must involve the whole of life, our minds, our souls and our physical and spiritual strength and we must also love our neighbours as ourselves.

Because God is love, when he is worshipped he reminds those who worship him of their neighbours. No offering therefore is acceptable to God from any who are not trying obediently to meet the needs of their neighbours.

Worship is the offering of that which is of most worth. Worship must begin in the knowledge of God which develops through the sense of his presence. We begin to worship when we recognise that presence. However, recognition of God's presence can only be achieved through obedience. We promise to strive with God's help to keep his holy will and commandments.

If we are trying to love God we shall try to love him with every part of life, with the mind, which we shall try to develop to learn as much as we can about him and his creation; with our souls because we can best reveal our love for him in the loving, unselfish, humble service we render to all mankind; with our strength which we shall try to develop because our bodies are temples of his Holy Spirit.

Commission

CONFIRM YOUR FAITH! To do this requires not only words, but actions. To confirm your faith means to become involved in what the Church is doing in the world. For each one of us, there is work to be done, power to do it and hope for the result of it.

The Work To Be Done

Jesus calls those who believe in him to do the works which he did, even greater works (John 14.12). Through those who confirm their faith in him, the works which he did in his physical body are to be done. The works are therefore greater because they are not confined to one physical body, but are done wherever there are believers. The promise of Jesus has been confirmed with the signs that have followed (Mark 16.20).

The works of Jesus while he was on earth were twofold. First they were works of teaching about God, with the proclamation of the good news that he had come to open the Kingdom of Heaven to all believers through the forgiveness of their sins. Secondly they were the works of healing and compassion.

The command of Jesus to his followers was and still is 'Go into all the world'. Every Christian is called to be a missionary wherever he or she may be. Not all believers are called to serve in places like Africa, Korea, India or Papua New Guinea, but all who confirm their faith should ask whether they may be so called to serve in such places as priests, nuns, deacons, builders, teachers, nurses, doctors, linguists or in some other way. However, it is the duty of every believer to support those who do serve in other lands as well as the work of the churches they serve by prayer and money.

It is also the duty of every believer to pray for the sick and to give practical help to all in need, wherever it is possible.

Power For The Work

The power through which Jesus worked was the Holy Spirit. 'God anointed Jesus of Nazareth with the Holy Spirit and with power, who went about doing good ...' said St Peter (Acts 10.38). The same power is promised to every believer.

'You shall receive power when the Holy Spirit is come upon you,' (Acts 1.8). Through this power, those who have confirmed their faith are made strong to do whatever work God calls them to do.

The Eternal Hope

When we confirm our faith, we also confirm our belief in the eternal hope and the glorious appearing of the great God and of our Saviour, Jesus Christ. Hope is the expectation of good. Hope is unseen. We pray in hope in the power of the Holy Spirit that in us and through us the Kingdom of God will come on earth as it is in heaven as we try to do his will on earth as it is done in heaven.

SOME PRAYERS

Confirmation Prayer (ASB 1980)

Defend, O Lord, your servants with your heavenly grace, that they may continue yours for ever, and daily increase in your Holy Spirit more and more, until they come to your everlasting kingdom. Amen.

St Francis of Assisi (1181–1226)

Lord, make me an instrument of your peace.
Where there is hatred, let me sow love;
where there is injury, pardon;
where there is doubt, faith;
where there is despair, hope;
where there is sadness, joy;
where there is darkness, light.

O Divine Master, grant that I may not so much
seek to be consoled, as to console;
not so much to be understood, as to understand;
not so much to be loved, as to love.
For it is in giving that we receive;
it is in pardoning that we are pardoned;
it is in dying that we are born again to eternal life.

St Teresa of Avila (1515–82)

Jesus Christ—
You have no body on earth but ours,
no hands but ours,
no feet but ours;   ours are the eyes
showing your compassion to the world;
ours are the feet with which you go about doing good;
ours are the hands with which you are to bless us now.

St Ignatius Loyola (1491–1556)

Teach us, good Lord, to serve you as you deserve;
to give and not to count the cost;
to fight and not to heed the wounds;
to toil and not to seek for rest;
to labour and not to ask for any reward,
but the knowledge that we do your will;
through Jesus Christ our Lord. Amen.

St Richard of Chichester (1197–1253)

Thanks be to you, my Lord, Jesus Christ,
for all the benefits which you have given me,
for all the pains and insults which you have borne
    for me:

O most merciful Redeemer, Friend and Brother;
may I know you more clearly,
love you more dearly,
and follow you more nearly,
day by day.

Sarum Primer (1558)

God be in my head and in my understanding;
God be in my eyes and in my looking;
God be in my mouth and in my speaking;
God be in my heart and in my thinking;
God be at my end and at my departing.

A prayer for those who have confirmed their Faith

We have not ceased to pray for you, asking that you may be filled with the knowledge of his will in all spiritual wisdom and understanding, to lead a life worthy of the Lord, fully pleasing to him, bearing fruit in every good work and increasing in the knowledge of God.

May you be strengthened with all power, according to his glorious might, for all endurance and patience with joy, giving thanks to the Father, who has qualified us to share in the inheritance of the saints in light.

(Colossians 1.9–12 R.S.V.)